Original title:
Slumber Safari: A Dreamy Adventure

Copyright © 2024 Creative Arts Management OÜ
All rights reserved.

Author: Theodore Sinclair
ISBN HARDBACK: 978-9916-90-498-5
ISBN PAPERBACK: 978-9916-90-499-2

Echoes of the Starlit Serenade

In the night, the stars align,
Whispers dance in silver light,
Echoes of dreams intertwine,
Songs of hope take flight.

Softly glows the moonlit sky,
Clouds drift like thoughts untold,
As the night begins to sigh,
Magic in the air unfolds.

Through the woods, a gentle breeze,
Carries tales of yesteryears,
Rustling leaves like lullabies,
Calm the heart and ease the fears.

Underneath this starlit quilt,
Love and laughter intertwine,
In the dark, a world is built,
Where the soul can truly shine.

Adventures in the Land of Drowsy Whispers

Close your eyes, embrace the dream,
In a world where shadows play,
Drowsy whispers softly stream,
Guiding you on your way.

Fields of clouds and rivers bright,
Wander where the fairies dwell,
Every moment feels just right,
In this land where wishes swell.

Floating boats on tea-stained seas,
Stars like lanterns in the mist,
Drift along with gentle ease,
Follow paths that can't be missed.

Every corner hides a tale,
Of lost dreams and secret skies,
In this realm, let worries pale,
Awake to see the magic rise.

An Odyssey Through Night's Caress

Beneath the moon's soft silver glow,
Whispers of night begin to flow.
Stars above in silent grace,
Guide my heart in night's embrace.

Through shadows deep, I take a stride,
With dreams and wishes as my guide.
The world transforms in dark's delight,
An odyssey through velvet night.

Reveries in a Twilight Lake

Where twilight wraps the world in gold,
Reflections dance, stories untold.
The water sparkles, a mystic sight,
A realm of dreams 'neath fading light.

Gentle ripples kiss the shore,
In this haven, I explore.
Whispers of the twilight breeze,
Invite my heart to find its ease.

Navigating the Starlit Paths

Across the sky, the stars align,
Guiding me through realms divine.
In the soft glow of cosmic art,
Navigating with an open heart.

Footsteps light, I wander free,
In the night's vast tapestry.
Each flicker tells a tale anew,
Of dreams and hopes that once I knew.

Dreamcatcher's Flight

In a web of threads, my dreams reside,
Held gently close, a trusted guide.
With every wish that takes to flight,
A dreamcatcher's dance in soft moonlight.

Through realms of slumber, I will soar,
Embracing magic, evermore.
In the realm where visions spin,
A journey deep, where dreams begin.

Treetops and Dream-Drops

In the hush of the twilight skies,
Treetops whisper to the night,
Dream-drops fall like stars in flight,
Cradling wishes and soft sighs.

Moonlight weaves through leafy seams,
Painting shadows on the ground,
While the forest softly sounds,
In a symphony of dreams.

The Slumbering Kingdom Unveiled

Beneath the veil of night's embrace,
A kingdom slumbers, lush and wide,
Stars like lanterns, guide the tide,
Of wishes whispered, secrets placed.

Gentle breezes start to play,
Rustling leaves in drowsy dance,
Awakening a golden chance,
For dreamers lost to drift away.

Nightfall Adventures in the Wild

As night creeps in, the wild awakes,
Creatures stir beneath the moon,
Echoes of the night-time tune,
Adventure calls, the heart it shakes.

Shadows stretch, and pathways gleam,
With every step, a story spins,
In the dark, where magic begins,
Awash with wonder, lost in dream.

A Dance with Sleepy Shadows

In twilight's glow, shadows embrace,
They twirl and sway, a soft ballet,
Underneath the stars' soft play,
In a world of tender grace.

As whispers wrap around the trees,
Sleepy whispers beckon near,
Drawing dreams, instilling cheer,
A dance with shadows on the breeze.

Reveries Among the Foliage

In the dappled light, shadows play,
Leaves whisper secrets, come what may.
Breezes carry tales, sweet and light,
As dreams unfold in the soft twilight.

Each branch holds stories, rich and wide,
Nature's canvas, where wonders bide.
Birds weave melodies with gentle grace,
Lost in reveries, time slows its pace.

Wandering Through Starry Whispers

Under the vast expanse of night,
Stars twinkle softly, a guiding light.
Moonbeams dance on the rippling sea,
Whispering tales of eternity.

Each step I take, the cosmos sighs,
Breath of the heavens, where magic lies.
In the stillness, dreams take flight,
Wandering through whispers, into the night.

The Enigma of the Nightingales

In the still of night, their songs arise,
Nightingales weave wonders in disguise.
Melodies echo, sweet notes blend,
A serenade that knows no end.

Beneath the moon's soft, silvery gaze,
Mysteries linger in the night's maze.
Each note a riddle, a heart's delight,
The enigma of love, in dark and light.

Chronicles of the Feathered Dreamers

In the morning mist, they take to flight,
Feathered dreamers dance in the light.
Each flutter tells of journeys wide,
Chronicles woven, with wings as their guide.

Through forests deep and valleys grand,
They sing of wonders across the land.
In every whisper, a story gleams,
Chronicles born from the heart of dreams.

The Hidden Echoes of Night

In shadows deep, the whispers sigh,
Secrets carried on a breeze,
Moonlight dances, shadows lie,
Echoes linger, soft with ease.

Stars alight in velvet skies,
Each a tale of dreams untold,
From the earth to where hope flies,
The night reveals its heart of gold.

Beneath the dark, a world awakes,
Gentle ripples wake the streams,
In the stillness, magic breaks,
And we drift into our dreams.

The night unfolds its serene art,
With every breath, a tender song,
Hidden echoes touch the heart,
In the dark, we all belong.

Enigma of the Enchanted Night

Through twilight mist, a path unfolds,
Where mysteries in silence blend,
The moon, a lantern made of gold,
Guiding souls where shadows bend.

Whispers twirl in the cool air,
With secrets held in velvet wraps,
Curious hearts drift without care,
Lost in time, the night entraps.

Branches sway with a gentle sway,
As starlight paints the dreams anew,
While echoes of the night seem to play,
In a dance of silver and blue.

In this land where wonders greet,
The enchantment hovers near and far,
Each heartbeat syncs with nature's beat,
As we reach out to touch a star.

Journey Through Dreamy Horizons

Beyond the hills, where shadows merge,
A journey starts with whispered sighs,
With every step, our hopes converge,
As dawn unfolds in gilded skies.

With every thought, a vision blooms,
A canvas painted by our dreams,
Where light dispels the night's cold glooms,
And reality is not what it seems.

Through valleys deep and rivers wide,
We wander on with spirits free,
In vivid hues, our hearts abide,
Embracing all we long to be.

At last, we find on horizons bright,
The beauty forged in twilight's hue,
A promise whispered by the night,
A journey shared, just me and you.

Nightlight in a Land of Wonder

In a realm where dreams take flight,
The stars ignite the velvet deep,
With every glimmer, pure delight,
Guarding wishes as we sleep.

The calm embraces every heart,
As night unfolds its velvet bow,
In every corner, magic starts,
Dancing softly, as if to show.

Whispers weave through trees so tall,
In rustling leaves, the night sings low,
A symphony of night's soft call,
In the glow of worlds aglow.

With every heartbeat, truth is spun,
A tapestry of dreams and light,
In this land where all is one,
Our hearts ignite the endless night.

A Whisper in the Waking Woods

In the forest where shadows play,
Leaves converse in soft ballet,
Birds serenade the dawn's embrace,
Nature's song in tranquil space.

Sunlight trickles through the green,
Casting glimmers, bright and clean,
A hush descends as day awakes,
Gentle whispers that nature makes.

Mossy paths and ancient trees,
Carry tales upon the breeze,
Every rustle, every sigh,
Hearts entwined beneath the sky.

In this moment, time stands still,
Nature bends to fit our will,
A whisper calls from deep within,
The waking woods, where dreams begin.

The Tranquil Dance of Dreams

In the stillness of the night,
Stars above, a guiding light,
Dreams take flight on whispered wings,
In the silence, magic sings.

Softly drifting through the haze,
Time dissolves in gentle ways,
Floating through a pastel sea,
Where all souls can wander free.

Moonlight spills on slumbered lands,
Casting shadows, soft like sands,
Every moment, fragile, rare,
In this dance, we breathe the air.

As the dawn begins to break,
From our dreams, we softly wake,
Grateful for the night's embrace,
For the calm, for the grace.

Voyage Beyond the Dreaming Dells

Sailing through the silver streams,
Chasing softly woven dreams,
Clouds like ships in twilight skies,
Where imagination flies.

Echoes of a distant place,
Time and space begin to grace,
Each moment feels like a sigh,
As the stars begin to cry.

Bursts of color dance around,
In this world, peace can be found,
Whispers of forgotten lore,
Guide us gently to the shore.

Here beneath the endless night,
We discover pure delight,
Voyage calls from deeper wells,
In the heart of dreaming dells.

Secrets of the Emerald Slumber

In the glade where shadows lie,
Nature's whispers float and sigh,
Emerald hues in soft repose,
Secrets wrapped in gentle prose.

Where the wildflowers weave their spell,
Hiding dreams, they know so well,
Every petal hides a tale,
Of adventures that set sail.

Crisp and clear, the evening air,
Cradles thoughts beyond compare,
In this realm of whispered night,
Sleep unfolds its purest light.

Secrets held in nature's art,
In the stillness, find your heart,
Emerald slumber, soft and deep,
In its arms, our dreams will keep.

Whispers of the Midnight Journey

In the stillness, echoes call,
Footsteps wander, shadows tall.
Stars above, a guiding light,
Whispers carry through the night.

Veils of mist, a soft embrace,
Secrets linger in their trace.
Each breath taken, dreams unfold,
Stories woven, softly told.

Voices dance on northern breeze,
Rustling leaves in ancient trees.
Paths obscured, yet hearts can see,
Whispers beckon, set us free.

The Land of Dreaming Beasts

In fields of gold, wild creatures play,
Tails a-wagging, night turns to day.
Eyes aglow with magic's gleam,
In this land, we dare to dream.

Moonlit skies, a gentle glow,
Wonders bloom where rivers flow.
Lions dance with gentle deer,
Whispers of joy fill the atmosphere.

A tapestry of dreams unfurled,
Each heartbeat, a new world.
Beasts of wonder, hearts entwined,
In this realm, our souls aligned.

Starlit Paths to Fantasia

Beneath the stars, a path begins,
Whispers of magic in the winds.
Fires glow, and spirits soar,
On this journey, we explore.

Each step glowing, bright and clear,
Fantasy waits, drawing near.
Unfolding tales, vibrant and bright,
Guiding us through the endless night.

A symphony of dreams resound,
In this land, our hopes abound.
Starlit paths, where few have trod,
Dancing with the warmth of God.

Chasing Moonlit Shadows

In silver beams, the shadows dart,
Chasing dreams, an eager heart.
Nighttime whispers, secrets share,
Every corner, magic's flare.

Softly gliding, breeze so light,
Through the veil of soft moonlight.
Wanderers seek what lies ahead,
In the stillness, fears are shed.

Elusive shapes of joy and fear,
Echoes of the night, so near.
Chasing shadows, we embrace,
All the wonders we can trace.

Shadows in the Misty Grove

In the grove, shadows dance,
Whispers of the night enhance.
Silhouettes in twilight's glow,
Secrets that the breezes blow.

Beneath the boughs where dreams entwine,
Silent echoes, soft and divine.
Moonlight drapes a silver cloak,
Nature's hush, a gentle spoke.

Footsteps fade on mossy ground,
In every crack, a mystery found.
Flickering lights, the fireflies' flight,
Lead us deeper into the night.

The mist enfolds like a tender sigh,
Where forgotten wishes drift and lie.
In this realm, where shadows play,
Lost in dreams, we wander away.

Radiant Reflections of the Nocturne

Stars above in velvet skies,
Twinkle bright with ancient ties.
Reflections in the stillness gleam,
Awakening the night's soft dream.

Luna's glow paints the serene,
Shadows cast a silvery sheen.
Every ripple tells a tale,
Of lovers lost, in moonlight pale.

The nightingale sings her sweet tune,
Under the watch of the shining moon.
In the hush, the world takes pause,
To admire beauty without cause.

A serenade of whispers flow,
As time dances, steady and slow.
In nocturnal embrace we sway,
Lost in reflections, we drift away.

Dreaming with the Wolves of Night

Beneath the moon's ethereal light,
Where the wild wolves roam in flight.
Their howls echo, a haunting call,
In dreams where shadows rise and fall.

The forest hums with secrets deep,
Where ancient spirits softly weep.
With each step, a story unfolds,
Of battles fought and legends told.

Mysterious eyes watch from the dark,
As we tread lightly, leaving our mark.
In unity, the pack takes flight,
Chasing echoes through the night.

Yet in stillness, a whisper sways,
As dreams weave through the starlit ways.
In the embrace of night's cool breath,
We find solace, even in death.

The Celestial Tapestry of Sleep

In the quiet realm of dreams,
Where nothing is quite as it seems.
Stars weave stories in the night,
Tapestries of sheer delight.

Gently floating, we drift away,
Into the night where shadows play.
Clouds of silver, soft as dreams,
Wrap us in their tender seams.

Through the cosmos, whispers flow,
Guiding hearts where starlight glows.
In this embrace, time stands still,
As the mind wanders where it will.

Each thread a journey, a tale untold,
In the fabric of night, we behold.
The universe cradles us tight,
In the celestial tapestry of sleep's light.

Awash in Luminescent Dreams

In the still of night, we drift away,
Beneath moonlit skies, where shadows play.
Whispers of stars, soft as a sigh,
In luminous realms, our spirits fly.

Dancing on beams of ethereal light,
Chasing the glow that feels so right.
With each heartbeat, colors gleam,
Awash in the tide of a tender dream.

Waves of dappled silence embrace,
Every twinkling spot, a sacred space.
The world beyond fades, a distant hue,
As we wade deeper, lost and true.

In this twilight realm, all worries cease,
Surrounded by love, wrapped in peace.
Awash in visions, forever bound,
In luminescent dreams, we are found.

Trail of the Starlit Spirits

Through the night, a gentle guide,
Starlit spirits walk by my side.
With every step, a story unfolds,
In whispers of light, their truth is told.

Glimmers of hope, they softly gleam,
Leading the lost through the night's dream.
On this trail where shadows blend,
Starlit spirits, a loving trend.

Underneath the vast, endless sky,
They beckon us with a knowing sigh.
In the dance of time, we find our way,
On the trail of magic that will not fray.

Farewell to doubts, the past shall fade,
In the embrace of the stars, unafraid.
With each glowing path, we chase our fate,
Starlit spirits guiding, oh, how great.

Dalmation Dreams and Haunted Hollows

In the hush of night, dark shadows creep,
Through haunted hollows, secrets seep.
Dalmation dreams in black and white,
Painted by moon's soft silver light.

Eerie echoes of laughter ring,
In the stillness, a ghostly wing.
Memory flickers, a candle's gleam,
In the depth of night, a haunting dream.

Whispers of stories long ago told,
In the haunted woods, we feel so bold.
With every rustle, a tale unfolds,
In Dalmation dreams, the spirit molds.

Together we wander, lost yet found,
Where secrets thrive, and fears abound.
Under the stars, the past ignites,
In haunted hollows, weaving our nights.

The Swirling Tides of Nighttime

Dark waves beckon with soothing care,
Swirling tides dance in the night air.
A symphony plays, soft and serene,
Whispers of dreams, so pure, so keen.

In the deep blue, shadows entwine,
Carried away on currents divine.
The moon's reflection, a guiding light,
Sailing us onward, through endless night.

Each moment flows like a gentle stream,
In the depths of darkness, we chase a dream.
Where tides embrace the sand's caress,
The swirling night sings of endlessness.

Through time and space, we drift along,
Carried by waves that weave our song.
In the still of night, our spirits glide,
On the swirling tides, where dreams abide.

Nocturnal Wanderlust

In the hush of the night, I roam,
Beneath a sky of velvet dome.
Where shadows dance and whispers call,
I trace the paths where dreamers fall.

Luminous stars, a guiding light,
Lead my heart through the endless night.
Each step unveils a tale untold,
In the embrace of night, I boldly hold.

The moon a lantern, softly glows,
Illuminating secrets no one knows.
With every breath, the world expands,
In nocturnal dreams, my spirit stands.

Wanderlust ignites the flame,
In every heart, a restless name.
Through winding trails on silent ground,
I find my truth, where voices sound.

Enchanted Visions Under Starlight

Beneath the stars, the world ignites,
With magic dancing, pure delights.
A canvas waits, both vast and bright,
As dreams unfold in soft moonlight.

Whispers linger in the breeze,
As ancient secrets find their keys.
Each twinkle tells a tale divine,
Under the gaze of cosmos' shine.

Glistening orbs, a serenade,
In twilight's hush, my doubts evade.
With wonders cast in silver glow,
In starlit dreams, my heart will flow.

Embrace this moment, feel the thrill,
As night enwraps the world so still.
In enchanted realms where shadows play,
Under starlight's spell, I'll always stay.

The Sleeping Jungle

In the cradle of leaves, silence lays,
Where the moonlight glimmers, softly sways.
A symphony of life in restful dreams,
The sleeping jungle whispers, it seems.

Muffled sounds, a tranquil song,
In shadows deep, where creatures throng.
The heartbeat of Earth, a gentle sigh,
As stars above, in glory, lie.

Gentle breezes kiss the night,
In slumber's warmth, the world feels right.
Each rustling leaf, a tale to tell,
In the jungle's embrace, I dwell.

Awake, yet lost in nature's flow,
In this sacred realm, my spirit glows.
The night cradles all in its tender care,
In the sleeping jungle, love lays bare.

Fantasia on a Moonbeam

A moonbeam glides through silver air,
Whispers of dreams, both light and rare.
Softly weaving through shadowed nights,
A fantastical dance, beyond our sights.

Timeless stories in glimmers told,
In fanciful realms where hearts unfold.
Each shimmer sparkles, a fleeting chance,
To twirl with stars in a cosmic dance.

The night unfolds a magic thread,
Woven with visions that gently spread.
In the glow of night, possibilities soar,
As life writes tales on mystic shore.

Fantasia weaves its endless scheme,
A tapestry bright, woven from dream.
In moonlit magic, I find my way,
Where fantasies linger and never fray.

Tranquil Trails of the Night

Under the moon's soft glow,
Whispers of the night do flow.
Stars above, a shimmering sea,
Guiding dreams, wild and free.

Footsteps hush on the dew-kissed ground,
In this calm, peace is found.
Crickets sing their lullabies,
Nature's song 'neath starlit skies.

Each breath a gentle, soothing breeze,
Rustling leaves in tranquil trees.
Night unfolds her velvet veil,
Tales of wonder softly sail.

Time stands still, shadows dance,
In this realm of sweet romance.
The heart beats slow, the mind takes flight,
Lost within tranquil trails of night.

A Sojourn in the Twilight Woods

In twilight's glow, the trees do sigh,
Softly speaking, not a lie.
Shadows stretch and dreams ignite,
Promising magic in the night.

Moss carpets paths of ancient lore,
Each step whispers of tales before.
Fireflies flit like stars on earth,
Illuminating secrets of birth.

Owls hoot softly, wise and keen,
Guardians of the woods unseen.
In the hush, the heart finds peace,
As the troubles of life slowly cease.

A journey here, where wonders blend,
In twilight's embrace, where dreams transcend.
The whispering winds, a soft caress,
In the woods, the soul finds rest.

Mysteries of the Midnight Realm

Beneath the stars, shadows creep,
Into the silence, secrets seep.
Moonlit whispers, stories unfold,
Ancient mysteries waiting to be told.

Fog drapes low, a shroud of dreams,
In the dark, nothing is as it seems.
Footsteps echo on paths unknown,
In the midnight realm, we roam alone.

A flicker of light, a breath on air,
Curiosity leads, but beware.
The night holds wonders, both dark and bright,
In this realm where shadows invite.

With each heartbeat, the night draws near,
Embrace the magic, shed the fear.
For in the depths, true wonders gleam,
In the midnight realm, we dare to dream.

Serenade of the Dreaming Beasts

When twilight descends on the sleeping ground,
A serenade stirs, a mystical sound.
Creatures of night rise from their rest,
In the hush, they sing, a timeless quest.

Owls serenade with their haunting calls,
While the moonlight dances on ancient walls.
Foxes prance with a whimsical grace,
In the shadows, they find their place.

Wolves howl to the echoing skies,
Filling the night with their soulful cries.
In the glade, where wildflowers steep,
The beasts of the night awaken from sleep.

Their harmonies weave through the velvety air,
A melody sweet, beyond compare.
In the heart of the night, we all feel,
The serenade of beasts, so surreal.

The Soothing Murmurs of Night

The moon whispers softly, a gentle beam,
Stars twinkle like secrets, lost in a dream.
Shadows dance lightly, on cool evening air,
Night wraps around us, a velvet affair.

Crickets play music, a delicate sound,
Breeze carries stories from all around.
In this calm moment, worries take flight,
Heart finds its rhythm in the soothing night.

Dreamers awaken, under the vast sky,
Painting their hopes on the canvas up high.
Each twinkling star shines with promise anew,
In the soothing murmurs, we start to renew.

The world fades away, it's just you and me,
Among the soft whispers, we're finally free.
Let the night cradle us, tender and light,
In the embrace of dreams, through the soothing night.

Wings of Imagination Under the Stars

Beneath the vast heavens, where dreams take flight,
Imagination soars, igniting the night.
With each twinkle above, ideas take wing,
In the heart of the dark, our fantasies sing.

Castles in clouds, and gardens of light,
We paint our own stories, all through the night.
Every star is a note in a symphonic breeze,
A melody carries, putting hearts at ease.

With wings made of dreams, we travel afar,
Guided by wonder, beneath each bright star.
Adventure awaits in the mind's endless sea,
In this realm of beauty, we set ourselves free.

So come, let us wander, hand in hand we'll roam,
In the wings of imagination, we find our home.
Under the stars shining bright in the skies,
Together we'll dream, where our true spirit lies.

The Lantern's Glow in the Dark Woods

In deep shadowed forests, where whispers abide,
A lantern is glowing, a warm, gentle guide.
Through the thick branches, a path we can find,
Illuminated dreams, by the light intertwined.

Footsteps are soft, like a hush in the night,
The lantern's glow flickers, a dance full of light.
Secrets of nature awaken and sigh,
Underneath the stars, where the old spirits lie.

Every flicker of flame tells a story untold,
Of wanderers lost and treasures of old.
In the veil of the twilight, the magic unfolds,
As the lantern's soft glow begins to hold.

So come, take a journey, through shadows we tread,
With the lantern beside us, there's nothing to dread.
In the dark woods, stories come alive,
Guided by the glow, we learn to thrive.

A Kaleidoscope of Dreaming Horizons

Horizons stretch wide, where colors collide,
A kaleidoscope spins, with dreams as our guide.
Each twist tells a tale, vibrant and bright,
Where day meets the dusk, painting soft light.

Mountains of wonder, valleys of grace,
In this canvas of life, we find our place.
Each step holds a dream, each breath a new hope,
In the rich tapestry, we learn how to cope.

The sky blushes pink, as day says goodbye,
Stars begin to shimmer, like jewels in the sky.
With visions of futures, so vivid and clear,
In this kaleidoscope, we conquer our fear.

Together we wander, through realms yet unseen,
Creating our stories, both silken and keen.
With every horizon, new dreams shall arise,
In the kaleidoscope world, we'll dance through the skies.

Embracing the Night's Secrets

Beneath a sky of shimmering stars,
Whispered tales of the moon's soft light,
Dancing shadows weave through the trees,
Embracing the night, we take flight.

Cool air wraps us in nature's hush,
Secrets linger where dreams take form,
The melody of silence sings,
In darkness, our spirits grow warm.

Echoes of laughter drift like mist,
Across the fields where wildflowers sway,
Night's embrace, so soft and sweet,
Guides us gently on our way.

Together we roam the velvet night,
Hand in hand, we share this view,
The world is ours, just us two,
In the night, our love feels brand new.

Fantasies Among the Drowsy Vines

Amidst the vines where dreams abide,
Enchanted whispers call our name,
Golden sunlight filters through,
Igniting vines in fiery flame.

Leaves rustle gently, secrets shared,
As shadows dance on the ground,
Fantasies blossom, wild and free,
In this haven, pure joy is found.

Beneath the canopies, time stands still,
With each breath, the world fades away,
Together we linger, lost in thoughts,
Among these vines, we choose to stay.

Embracing the magic of lazy days,
Where laughter twirls with gentle sighs,
In this dream, we find our place,
Fantasies bloom under azure skies.

Twilight-Touched Fantasies

Twilight descends with a painted sky,
Brush strokes of purple and gold,
Nestled in dreams, we weave our tales,
In this hour, our hearts unfold.

Stars awaken, one by one,
Casting their glow on the gentle stream,
We drift softly on whispered winds,
Caught in the web of a twilight dream.

The world is hushed, in reverence waits,
As magic dances in the dim light,
Hand in hand, we chase the stars,
In fantasies touched by the night.

Moments stretch like shadows long,
In the fading glow, we find our song,
With every heartbeat, we belong,
In twilight's embrace, forever strong.

Explorations in a Dreamy Wilderness

In the depths of the wild, we wander free,
Where dreams and reality intertwine,
Soft whispers guide us through the trees,
In this world, our spirits align.

Each step unveils a new surprise,
As petals fall like gentle rain,
Mysteries hidden in the thicket,
Calling us to explore again.

The brook hums a tune, sweet and clear,
While sunlight dances on the stream,
Together we chase the fleeting light,
In this wilderness, we find our dream.

Echoing laughter fills the air,
We dive deep into nature's embrace,
Adventures await, just beyond the bend,
In this dreamy wilderness, we find our place.

Whimsical Flights Across the Moon

On silver beams we glide and soar,
Through clouds that dance and spirits roar.
The gentle night, our canvas deep,
In whispers shared, our secrets keep.

With laughter bright, we paint the skies,
In twirling waltzes, dreams arise.
Beneath the stars, our hearts take flight,
In endless joy, we chase the light.

From craters deep to lunar glow,
We craft our tales, where wonders flow.
With playful hearts and open minds,
The universe our joy unwinds.

In whimsical views where wishes bloom,
We dance unharmed, we banish gloom.
Together lost, yet always found,
In flights that echo, love all around.

Secrets Beneath the Dreaming Canopy

Beneath the leaves, the shadows play,
In secrets whispered, night holds sway.
The roots entwined, a tale to weave,
In twilight's glow, we dare believe.

A soft breeze carries stories old,
Of hidden paths and dreams untold.
In twinkling light, the fireflies glint,
As magic dances, hearts imprint.

We lay upon the mossy floor,
In nature's hug, our spirits soar.
With every sigh the silence breaks,
In harmony, the stillness wakes.

Beneath the stars, our dreams parade,
In whispered tones, our fears allayed.
The canopy, a blanket wide,
In nature's hush, we both confide.

Paths of Celestial Silence

In twilight's hush, where shadows blend,
The path ahead has no clear end.
With stardust trails and a silken breeze,
Our souls entwined among the trees.

Each step a hush, a sacred sound,
In stillness deep, our hearts rebound.
The universe, a canvas vast,
In silence deep, our dreams are cast.

We wander forth, the night our guide,
In whispers soft, where secrets hide.
The cosmos sings its dulcet tone,
In paths celestial, we are not alone.

As thoughts drift deep into the night,
We find our peace in purest light.
In silence shared, our spirits climb,
On paths of stars, eternal rhyme.

The Quiet Realm of Hidden Dreams

In corners dim, where shadows dwell,
A realm exists that we can't tell.
With hidden dreams and starlit skies,
The heart's true wish forever lies.

In gentle whispers, tales arise,
Of joyful laughter, soft replies.
Each secret thought a treasure bright,
In quiet realms, we chase the light.

Through silken threads of hopes untold,
We find our stories, brave and bold.
With every heartbeat, every sigh,
In this still place, our spirits fly.

So linger here, where silence reigns,
In quiet realms, we feel love's chains.
Together lost, together found,
In hidden dreams, our hearts unbound.

The Adventure of Forgotten Dreams

In a land where shadows play,
Forgotten dreams drift far away.
Whispered secrets in the breeze,
Awake the heart from silent freeze.

Tales of journeys yet untold,
Adventurers brave, both young and old.
Chasing echoes through the night,
Guided by stars, a distant light.

With each step, new paths unfold,
Stories waiting to be bold.
Fellow travelers by your side,
Together through the dark, we glide.

In the twilight, dreams ignite,
Flames of courage burning bright.
The adventure calls to every soul,
A quest for dreams that makes us whole.

Dances with Dreaming Shadows

In twilight's grace, they take their form,
Shadows twirl in a mystic storm.
Steps of laughter, whispers low,
In the dance where moonbeams flow.

Drifting softly through the night,
Partners lost in sheer delight.
Every movement, another tale,
A silent song on winds so pale.

Hues of silver, hints of blue,
They weave a dream for me and you.
Cloaked in darkness, they invite,
Swaying gently, hearts take flight.

In this realm where visions gleam,
Lies a world born from a dream.
Hand in hand with shadows sweet,
In this dance, our souls repeat.

Nurtured by the Night's Embrace

Beneath the stars, in silence deep,
The night wraps dreams in gentle keep.
A lullaby of softest light,
Guiding hearts till morning bright.

Embraced by silence, secrets sigh,
Whispers of love drift through the sky.
In shadows' arms, we find our place,
Nurtured deep in night's embrace.

Every moment, a tender kiss,
In darkness, we unravel bliss.
Held by time, as it gentle sways,
Lost to dreams, the night obeys.

Wrapped in comfort, fears release,
In this stillness, we find peace.
Together under the moon's gaze,
Nurtured by the night's embrace.

Surreal Treasures Awaiting

In a realm where colors blend,
Surreal dreams begin to mend.
Artifacts of the mind's delight,
Treasures gleam in soft moonlight.

Wonders hidden, take your time,
Each moment feels like a rhyme.
Fragments scattered, paths to find,
Unlocking secrets of the mind.

Through the mist, we take our flight,
Chasing visions into the night.
Every heartbeat brings us near,
To treasures rich, both rare and sheer.

In this dance of chance and fate,
Surreal treasures await our state.
Embrace the magic yet untold,
In dreams' embrace, we dare be bold.

The Gentle Whisper of Midnight Mysteries

In the stillness of the night,
Soft secrets dance in silver light.
Stars twinkle like dreams unspun,
Echoes of lore, their stories run.

The moon drapes shadows, deep and wide,
Guiding lost souls with quiet pride.
Each rustling leaf, a tale to tell,
Wrapped in the night's soothing spell.

Ghostly whispers brush the air,
Every heartbeat, a silent prayer.
In the grasp of twilight's fold,
Mysteries of night gently unfold.

With every sigh, the dawn is near,
But time stands still, and we remain here.
To wander through realms of dreams untold,
In the midnight's charm, we are consoled.

Chasing Shadows Through Dreamscapes

In the realm where visions play,
Shadows dance and softly sway.
Through the mist, we wander free,
Chasing echoes of what could be.

Each whisper lures us deeper still,
As waking thoughts begin to fill.
Dreams unravel in hues so bright,
Guided by the shimmering light.

Fleeting moments, a tapestry,
Woven with hopes and reverie.
Navigating paths of the heart,
In this place, we'll never part.

Let the shadows lead the way,
Through the night until the day.
In the chase of dreams, we find,
Endless worlds that bind our minds.

The Twilight Reverie's Lull

As daylight fades to pastel skies,
The whispers of twilight softly rise.
In the embrace of the dusk's gentle sway,
Dreams begin their tender play.

Stars awaken with a sparkling glow,
Painting the night with secrets to know.
With every sigh, the universe sighs,
In stillness, wonder multiplies.

Crickets sing in a soothing tune,
Under the watch of the rising moon.
Rest your thoughts in this cozy reprieve,
As the twilight weaves its magic weave.

In reverie's arms, we gently fall,
Safe and sound, we heed the call.
For in this lull, dreams take flight,
Wrapped in the warmth of the night.

Quest in the Realm of Dreams

On the edge of sleep's embrace,
A quest begins in a timeless place.
With every blink, the world transforms,
New visions rise in endless forms.

Through valleys deep and mountains high,
Chasing wonders beneath the sky.
Each heartbeat echoes in cosmic dance,
In the realm of dreams, we take our chance.

Guided by starlight's gentle gleam,
We unravel the threads of every dream.
With courage stitched in every seam,
We journey far, our spirits beam.

Awake or dreaming, time stands still,
In this quest, we find our will.
For every step in dreams we tread,
Brings us closer to where we're led.

Adventures in Twilight's Embrace

In the hues where shadows play,
Whispers echo, night takes sway.
Curious hearts venture near,
Chasing dreams with little fear.

Stars awaken, softly gleam,
Guiding paths through twilight's theme.
Moments linger, time seems still,
Adventures beckon, hearts will thrill.

Misty trails and hidden streams,
Open up to quiet dreams.
Nature calls with gentle grace,
In the twilight's warm embrace.

Laughter dances on the breeze,
As the night begins to tease.
Hand in hand, we roam the night,
In adventures born of light.

The Gentle Call of the Moonlit Wild

Beneath the stars, the wildflowers sway,
A gentle call beckons, soft as day.
Moonlit paths where shadows hide,
Nature's secrets, ours to bide.

Crickets sing their soothing tune,
Guided by the watchful moon.
Whispers brush against our skin,
In the wild, our hearts begin.

Trees embrace the starlit air,
Holding stories, secrets rare.
Let us wander, side by side,
In the night, where dreams reside.

Hold your breath, feel the night,
Every moment, pure delight.
The wild calls with gentle grace,
Inviting us to lose our pace.

Moonlit Souls and Whispering Winds

In the night's soft, tender light,
Moonlit souls take silent flight.
Whispering winds through leaves do weave,
Carrying tales of those who believe.

Stars above, a scattered chart,
Guiding dreams, igniting hearts.
In this realm of silver glow,
Every wish begins to flow.

With every breeze, a promise made,
In the beauty of twilight's shade.
Hand in hand, we venture far,
Chasing echoes of a star.

Let the night our spirits mold,
In the warmth, we'll be consoled.
For in this hush, we find our way,
Moonlit souls, come what may.

The Forest of Forgotten Dreams

In the heart of the ancient wood,
Lies a place misunderstood.
Whispers echo through the trees,
Carrying tales upon the breeze.

Leaves remember every sigh,
In this realm where dreams don't die.
Lost ambitions gently twine,
In the shadows, hopes align.

Mossy stones and aged vines,
Guarding secrets, hidden signs.
Every step, a story told,
In the forest, dreams unfold.

So let us stroll through twilight's door,
In the peace of evermore.
For in this space of whispered seams,
We awaken forgotten dreams.

The Sleepy Explorer's Quest

In twilight's glow, the stars ignite,
A winding path, the dreams take flight.
With whispered tales of distant lands,
An explorer's heart in slumber stands.

Through valleys deep and hills so high,
Where moonlight dances, shadows fly.
With every breath, adventure calls,
As night unfolds, the mystery enthralls.

The map is drawn in stardust's weave,
A secret trove for those who believe.
With every step in dreams we tread,
An uncharted realm that lies ahead.

Awake or asleep, the quest endures,
For wonder lies in heart's own cures.
So with a smile, the journey starts,
The sleepy explorer, chasing hearts.

Night's Gentle Serenade

In the calm of night, a lullaby,
Soft whispers drift through the midnight sky.
The moonlit glow, a tender scene,
Where dreams are born and hearts convene.

A symphony of crickets sings,
Wrapped in the warmth that twilight brings.
The stars above, they blink and play,
Guiding the lost to their own way.

With every sigh, the breezes flow,
Caressing fields of fresh-cut snow.
Night's gentle hand embraces all,
In stillness watches as shadows fall.

As dawn approaches, the song will fade,
Yet in our hearts, the serenade.
With every night, the magic stays,
A memory woven in twilight's haze.

Wonders Beyond the Waking World

Past the veils of sleep, the wonders gleam,
In realms where thoughts can freely dream.
Mysteries await in colors bold,
Stories untold, treasures unfold.

Through sapphire oceans and amber skies,
A tapestry where imagination flies.
Each heartbeat drip, a whispering muse,
Igniting echoes of paths to choose.

In fields of stars, where shadows blend,
The waking world begins to bend.
A gentle shift, a timeless swirl,
Unraveling dreams in a waking whirl.

Beyond the light, where wonders dwell,
We find the magic, we hear the bell.
As dawn breaks open with life's embrace,
We carry the dreams to lighter space.

A Voyage Through Velvet Skies

In velvet skies, the stars arise,
With every breath, the cosmos sighs.
A ship of dreams on starlit seas,
Sails unfurled in the midnight breeze.

Galaxies swirl in a dance divine,
Casting wishes on the pathways of time.
With every heartbeat, the journey flows,
In the silence of night, the courage grows.

The constellations greet our gaze,
Bringing whispers of celestial praise.
Through nebulae bright, by comet's tail,
We navigate the cosmic sail.

With each dawn, we return once more,
From the velvet skies to the earthly shore.
But within our hearts, the voyage stays,
A tapestry woven in twilight's rays.

Echoes of a Lullaby Forest

The whispers of the trees, so sweet,
In shadows where the soft hearts meet.
A tranquil breeze drifts through the night,
Wrapping dreams in silver light.

Beneath the moon's gentle gaze they sway,
Inviting wanderers to gently stay.
Each rustling leaf sings a tune,
Cradled close beneath the moon.

The brook hums softly, a lullaby's thread,
Through fern and flower, where spirits tread.
With every step, a story weaves,
In the cradle of the forest leaves.

As stars peer down, in silence they gleam,
Guardians watching over the dream.
Nature's arms hold us, safe and tight,
In the peaceful lap of night.

A Journey Through the Dreamscape

Upon the waves of slumber's tide,
Where all the hidden thoughts reside.
With every breath, the world transforms,
Into a realm where magic swarms.

Clouds take shapes of thoughts untold,
Mysterious journeys, brave and bold.
A landscape painted in vibrant hues,
Where one can wander, lose the blues.

In shadows deep, the phantoms play,
Guiding lost souls along the way.
Each whispering thought, a glowing star,
Illuminates the path afar.

As dawn approaches, dreams will fade,
Yet in the heart, their echo stayed.
For every journey leaves a trace,
In the canvas of the dreamscape.

The Starlit Playground of Fantasies

Where moonbeams dance on silken grass,
And laughter echoes as moments pass.
Children of the night come to play,
In a world where shadows softly sway.

Bright constellations twinkle above,
In this sanctuary of dreams and love.
With every step, a new tale spun,
Under the watch of the midnight sun.

Magic lingers in the cool night air,
Whispers of wishes spun with care.
Each flicker of light a promise made,
In this playground where hopes invade.

As the stars begin their gentle descent,
Time pauses in this firmament.
In the heart of the night, we find release,
In the starlit playground, we find peace.

The Velvet Night's Embrace

Wrapped in the cloak of velvet night,
Where shadows dance in gentle light.
Soft whispers float on a moonlit sea,
Cradling hearts in serenity.

A tapestry woven of dreams and sighs,
Where secrets linger beneath the skies.
With every breath, the night unfolds,
In the warmth of stories begging to be told.

Stars sprinkle joy, like diamonds bright,
Guiding lost souls in their flight.
A symphony sings in the cool, crisp air,
As time drifts gently in this atmosphere.

The night, a canvas of endless grace,
Holds the world in a tender embrace.
In its quiet depths, we come to find,
A haven of peace for the restless mind.

The Enchanted Slumber Voyage

In the hush of night, dreams unfold,
A ship of clouds, sails of gold.
Stars are lanterns, softly gleam,
Whispers drift in a moonlit stream.

Through the velvet skies we glide,
On waves of sleep, we take our ride.
The world below fades from sight,
In the embrace of endless night.

Voices call from lands unknown,
In slumber's realm, we find our own.
Every heartbeat a gentle sway,
Guiding us through the dreams at play.

With every star, a tale is spun,
In the journey, we become one.
Awake or asleep, our spirits soar,
Enchanted slumbers forevermore.

Creatures of the Dreamscape

Amidst the shadows, creatures creep,
In the depths of the dreamers' sleep.
Whiskered beings with eyes aglow,
Dance in the twilight, soft and slow.

Wings of colors, bright and bold,
Stories of magic waiting to be told.
They flit through mists, on silken threads,
Weaving dreams where the brave dare tread.

In secret glades and twilight streams,
They summon forth our wildest dreams.
With every step, their laughter sings,
Enchanting hearts with the joy it brings.

From corner to corner, the dreamscape thrives,
With creatures of wonder, where magic thrives.
In harmony, they share their lore,
Inviting us to explore and soar.

Forests of Whispering Dreams

In the twilight woods, dreams softly speak,
Among the trees, where shadows peek.
Leaves like pages turn in the night,
Telling tales of forgotten flight.

Moonlit paths lead us to stare,
At glimmers of magic hanging in air.
Whispers echo, secrets take flight,
In these forests, all feels right.

From roots below to branches above,
Every creature shares its love.
The rustling leaves, a soft refrain,
Calling us to dance in the rain.

In this realm of the sacred and still,
Dreams intertwine with the heart's will.
As we wander through the night's embrace,
We find ourselves in this sacred space.

A Tapestry of Nocturnal Adventures

Threads of silver, woven tight,
Kaleidoscope visions of the night.
Adventures spring from every seam,
A tapestry shaped by the dream.

Horizon blushes, stars appear,
In the shadowed corners, we draw near.
Every stitch tells a story bold,
Of escapades waiting to be told.

Beneath the sky, we find our flight,
Exploring realms bathed in soft light.
With every dream that flutters by,
We gather courage, we learn to fly.

In this fabric of time and space,
Nocturnal wonders we embrace.
As the dawn beckons, dreams take flight,
Together we weave the threads of night.

Echoes of the Lullaby Journey

In twilight's hush, the whispers flow,
Of gentle dreams that softly glow.
With every heartbeat, tales arise,
A serenade beneath the skies.

Through valleys deep, the shadows play,
In rhythmic waves, they dance and sway.
The moonlight guides, a silver thread,
Where echoes linger, hearts are fed.

The stars align in silent song,
As wanderers drift, where they belong.
In every note, the world is spun,
A lullaby until the dawn.

With every sigh, illusions weave,
As secrets in the night, we believe.
The journey lingers, sweet and bright,
In echoes soft, we trust the night.

Shadows of the Slumbering Wild

In fields of green, the shadows creep,
Where nature's heart begins to sleep.
With every rustle, dreams take flight,
In silent woods, cloaked deep in night.

Whispers of creatures roam the air,
As starlit paths lead us somewhere.
The wild holds secrets, old and wise,
In slumber's grip, the world complies.

Beneath the boughs, a hush prevails,
As stories dance on hidden trails.
The lull of night, a gentle sigh,
Where shadows dwell, we softly lie.

In every heartbeat, wild and free,
The dreams reflect our mystery.
A realm where darkness finds its grace,
In slumbering wild, we find our place.

Moonbeams over Dreamy Shores

On sandy shores, the moonlight calls,
As silver tides embrace, enthralls.
With every wave, a tale untold,
In whispers soft, the night unfolds.

The ocean hums a lullaby,
As stars cascade from velvet sky.
In rhythmic motion, hearts will sway,
While dreams like shells upon the bay.

Beneath the glow of cosmic light,
We gather dreams, both bold and bright.
With every heartbeat, love's refrain,
In moonlit waltz, we lose our pain.

Together here, the world dissolves,
In dances sweet, our souls resolve.
On dreamy shores, where shadows blend,
The moonbeams kiss, and night won't end.

Fantastic Beasts in the Twilight

In twilight's grasp, the wonders rove,
Fantastic beasts in realms we wove.
With eyes aglow, they softly tread,
On paths where only dreams have led.

A dragon's roar, a phoenix's cry,
In enchanted lands, they soar and fly.
With every flutter, tales arise,
In twilight's magic, under skies.

The whispers of the woods unite,
As creatures bask in fading light.
Each step a dance, with hearts entwined,
In fantastic realms, freedom's defined.

With stardust trails, they lead the way,
In twilight's hold, we long to stay.
In dreams we wander, wild and free,
With fantastic beasts, just you and me.

Fantastical Journeys in Sleep's Embrace

In dreams we sail on silver seas,
Where stars align with whispered pleas.
A journey starts in the hush of night,
Guided by the moon's soft light.

Through forests deep and skies so vast,
We chase the echoes of the past.
Each step reveals a world anew,
Wrapped in twilight's gentle hue.

With every turn, the magic spins,
As laughter dances on the winds.
In slumber's arms, our spirits fly,
Beyond the realms where shadows lie.

Upon the dawn, we greet the day,
With dreams that taught us how to play.
Though morning comes with golden rays,
In sleep's embrace, our hearts will stay.

A Quest for Midnight Whispers

When twilight calls with a velvet sigh,
We gather dreams that softly lie.
Through hidden paths, we seek the phrase,
Of whispered secrets in the haze.

Beneath the glow of a silver star,
We roam the night, our souls ajar.
With every breath, the magic brews,
In quest of tales we long to choose.

Like fireflies dancing in the breeze,
We chase the night with hearts at ease.
On wings of shadows, we delve so deep,
Into the realms where visions sleep.

As dawn approaches, the whispers fade,
Yet in our hearts, their echoes made.
For every quest must find its end,
But in our dreams, the night will blend.

Caves of the Sleeping Giant

In caverns dark, where echoes dwell,
Lies the tale yet left to tell.
A giant sleeps in shadows deep,
Guarding secrets lost in sleep.

With lanterns bright, we venture near,
Through stalactites that glisten clear.
Each step a heartbeat in the stone,
In the sleeping giant's throne.

The walls are painted with forgotten lore,
Of battles fought and ancient war.
In silent whispers, the past unfolds,
In every corner, a story holds.

And when we leave this hidden place,
We carry dreams of the giant's grace.
For every shadow hides a spark,
In the caves where magic hark.

Starlit Beds and Cloudy Trails

Beneath the stars, we lay our feet,
On paths of mist, our journey sweet.
A starlit bed, our dreams do weave,
In cloudy trails, we softly believe.

The night sky whispers a tale of old,
Of dreams and wishes, brave and bold.
With every breath, the cosmos calls,
As laughter dances through the halls.

In twilight's arms, the world is wide,
With every star, our hopes abide.
As morning break, the dreams we've spun,
Will linger long, the night not done.

We rise anew with hearts aglow,
From starlit beds, we choose to grow.
For every night holds magic's key,
In cloudy trails, we wander free.

The Realm of Nighttime Revelry

In shadowed halls where whispers flow,
The moonlight dances, soft and low.
Laughter twinkles in the air,
A secret world without a care.

Masked figures glide with silent grace,
Joyful spirits, a warm embrace.
Each heartbeat echoes, a vibrant song,
In this realm where we belong.

Stars above in a velvet sky,
We lose ourselves, let dreams fly high.
With every turn, the night takes flight,
In the realm of nighttime delight.

As dawn approaches, shadows fade,
But memories of joy won't trade.
In our hearts, the echoes stay,
Until night comes to claim the day.

The Hidden Groves of Reverie

Beyond the trails where few have trod,
Lie groves of dreams, a sacred nod.
Whispers of leaves, a gentle sigh,
In secret places, souls can fly.

Sunbeams dance through tangled vines,
Painting paths where magic shines.
Flowing waters sing their tune,
Beneath the watchful eye of the moon.

Each step reveals a tale untold,
Of fleeting moments, treasures bold.
In the hush of nature's grace,
We find ourselves in this embrace.

So linger here in twilight's glow,
In hidden groves where dreams can flow.
With open hearts, let wonder thrive,
In the sacred space where we're alive.

Clouds that Carry Secrets

Drifting softly, white and gray,
Clouds whisper secrets of the day.
Veils of mystery, soft and light,
Kissing the earth, a gentle flight.

They cradle stories, lost in time,
Songs of nature, pure and rhyme.
Beneath their shadows, we await,
To catch the dreams they bring our fate.

As they wander, shift, and sway,
Painting skies in shades of gray.
They hold the laughter, tears we've shed,
In every glimpse, the words unsaid.

So look above, with open eyes,
For clouds that hold the softest sighs.
In every puffy, fleeting seam,
Resides the beauty of a dream.

Dreams in the Garden of Stars

In the garden where starlight grows,
Dreams are whispered soft and slow.
Petals glimmer, hopes take flight,
In twilight's embrace, pure delight.

Moonlit paths weave through the trees,
Carved by breezes, echoing ease.
Each bloom cradles a wish so dear,
As cosmos twinkles, drawing near.

Quiet moments wrapped in night,
Glistening visions burning bright.
In this haven, we align,
With every heartbeat, love defines.

So gather 'round where wishes bloom,
In the heart of night's sweet room.
In the garden of stars we see,
The dreams we hold, forever free.

The Dreamweaver's Trail

In starry skies where shadows play,
The Dreamweaver walks at end of day.
Threads of silver, softly spun,
Woven whispers, dreams begun.

Softly glowing, the lanterns sway,
Guiding souls who've lost their way.
On the path of hope they tread,
Finding solace in words unsaid.

With every starlit step they take,
A lullaby for all hearts to wake.
In the tapestry of night they find,
The secrets of the dreamers entwined.

For every wish upon a star,
The Dreamweaver knows just who you are.
A journey led by heart and mind,
On this trail, true peace they find.

Beyond the Velvet Veil of Night

Beneath the velvet veil of night,
Stars ignite with endless light.
Dreams take flight on whispers soft,
Carried where the shadows loft.

In the hush of midnight's grace,
The moonlight casts a silver lace.
Stories told in silence clear,
Echoes of the ones we hold dear.

Lost in twilight's gentle fold,
Secrets of the heart unfold.
Beyond the veil where wishes soar,
Lies the magic at night's core.

For every moment spent in awe,
Life reveals its hidden law.
Embrace the night and let it guide,
To deeper dreams where hopes abide.

Whispers of the Moonlit Voyage

Sailors of dreams, on waters still,
Whispers beckon with a soothing thrill.
The moonlit path, a shimmering guide,
Carving tales where shadows abide.

Stars play a melody soft and sweet,
As each wave groans beneath their feet.
Journeying forth through endless skies,
Leaving echoes of silent sighs.

In the depths of night, secrets flow,
Navigating where heartbeats glow.
With every stroke, a promise made,
The moonlit voyage shall never fade.

Through twilight's gaze and dawn's embrace,
A world awaits in sacred space.
Whispers weave a tale of old,
An odyssey of dreams retold.

The Dreamweaver's Path

Upon the path where dreams reside,
The Dreamweaver walks with quiet pride.
With every step, a tale unfolds,
Crafting futures in whispers bold.

Along the way, the colors dance,
Inviting souls to take a chance.
From light to dark, from day to night,
Guiding hearts to find their light.

In the quiet, seeds of hope grow,
Nurtured by the moon's soft glow.
The way is long, but never bleak,
For each heart finds what it seeks.

So take the path, let dreams ignite,
Embrace the journey, hold on tight.
In the tapestry of time, we weave,
The Dreamweaver's magic, we believe.

Milton Keynes UK
Ingram Content Group UK Ltd.
UKHW021928011224
451790UK00005B/62